I Have a Dream

THURGOOD MARSHALL

A Dream of Justice for All

By Stuart A. Kallen

Published by Abdo & Daughters, 4940 Viking Drive Suite 622, Edina, Minnesota 55435.

Library bound edition distributed by Rockbottom Books, Pentagon Tower, P.O. Box 36036, Minneapolis, Minnesota 55435.

Cover photo -   Bettmann
Interior photos - Bettmann

Edited by Rosemary Wallner

Kallen, Stuart A., 1955-
    Thurgood Marshall: a dream of justice for all / written by Stuart
A. Kallen.
            p. cm. -- (I Have a Dream)
Includes bibliographical references and index.
Summary: A biography of the first African-American Supreme Court justice, who worked at making civil rights possible for all Americans.
ISBN 1-56239-258-1
1. Marshall, Thurgood, 1908-1993 -- Juvenile literature. 2. United States. Supreme Court -- Biography -- Juvenile literature. 3. Judges -- United States -- Biography -- Juvenile literature. 4. Civil rights -- United States -- History -- Juvenile literature. [1. Marshall, Thurgood, 1908-1993. 2. Judges. 3. United States, Supreme Court -- Biography. 4. Afro-Americans.-- Biography.] I. Title. II. Series.
KF8745.M34K35   1993
347.73'2634--dc20
    [B]
                                          93-8333
                                              CIP
                                              AC

TABLE OF CONTENTS

Chapter **1**

Growing

Up

Smart

and

Tough

*I*t was the morning of June 13, 1967, when U.S. Attorney General Ramsey Clark strode into the office of Thurgood Marshall in Washington, D.C. Marshall was the first African American to hold the office of solicitor general. Marshall's job was to represent the United States in cases before the Supreme Court.

"What are you doing this morning?" asked Clark.

"At 11 o'clock I've got to go up to the White House and talk to some students," replied Marshall.

"Well, go up there at 10:45 instead and go to the Oval Office," Clark told Marshall. The Oval Office was the office of President Lyndon Banes Johnson (LBJ).

"What's it about?" Marshall inquired.

"I don't know," Clark answered.

He told Marshall to get inside the White House without the press seeing him.

When Marshall finally arrived at Johnson's office, he waited until the president spoke. "You know something, Thurgood?" asked LBJ.

"No, sir, what's that?"

"I'm going to put you on the Supreme Court," Johnson drawled.

"Oh, yippee," said Marshall. "What did you say?"

"That's it, " said Johnson.

"O.K., sir." That was all Marshall could think of saying.

Johnson had the press waiting in the Rose Garden outside his office. Marshall was whisked out to the assembled crowd while LBJ made the announcement. Thurgood Marshall would be the first African-American to sit on the Supreme Court!

President Lyndon Johnson named Thurgood Marshall the first African-American Supreme Court Justice.

Back in the Oval Office, Marshall asked the president if he could call his wife, Sissie. He wanted to tell her the news before she heard it on TV.

"You mean you haven't told Sissie yet?" LBJ asked Marshall.

"No, how could I. I've been with you the whole time."

So Marshall called Sissie.

"Sissie, are you sitting down?" Marshall asked his wife.

"No," she said.

"You better sit down," Marshall told her.

She did. Marshall handed the phone to LBJ.

"Sissie," said the president. "I just put your husband on the Supreme Court."

"I'm glad I'm sitting down," said Sissie.

Then LBJ turned to Marshall, "I guess this is the end of our friendship."

Marshall knew that members of the Supreme Court often had to fight against presidents. "Yep. Just about. Be no more of that," he replied.

"Well, that's the way I want it," replied LBJ.

And that's the way it was.

"A PRETTY TOUGH GUY"

*I*t was a long journey for Thurgood Marshall from the rough-and-tumble back alleys of Baltimore to a seat on the nation's highest court. Not a journey so much of miles, but of long hours reading law books and tough fights in hostile courtrooms. Most importantly, across barriers erected by racism. But Marshall was always a tough guy ready for scrappy battles. And he came from a long line of proud people who fought tough battles in their day and in their way.

Thurgood Marshall was born on July 2, 1908, in West Baltimore, Maryland. His great-great grandfather on his mother's side had been a slave, brought to America in the mid-1800s. "His polite descendants like to think he came from the cultured tribes in Sierra Leone," Marshall recalled. "But we all know that he really came from the toughest part of the Congo." (The Congo is now called the Republic of Zaire.)

Marshall said his great-great grandfather was so surly that his owner set him free just to get rid of him. Setting a slave free was very unusual; in the 1800s a slave owner could legally kill a rebellious slave. The freed slave settled down on a farm not too far away and lived out his days in relative peace.

Marshall's grandfather on his father's side was an ex-slave known only as "Marshall." When he became a soldier in the Civil War, he was told he needed a first name and a last name. He chose to be called "Thoroughgood" Marshall because he felt he was good through and through. After helping in the fight to free the slaves, Thoroughgood married a woman named Annie and opened a grocery store in Baltimore.

Thurgood Marshall was named after his grandfather, but, he said, "by the time I was in second grade, I got tired of spelling all that and shortened it."

Marshall's grandfather on his mother's side was named Isiah Olive Branch Williams. Although the olive branch is a symbol for peace, Isiah was another tough man who fought for his rights. In the 1870s, Isiah organized Baltimore's blacks to protest police brutality against the city's African-Americans. This was done at a time when racist groups like the Ku Klux Klan (KKK) often killed defiant blacks.

Isiah Williams' daughter, Norma Arica, married William Canfield Marshall in 1904. They had two sons, William Aubrey in 1904 and Thurgood in 1908. By the time Thurgood was born, the family lived in a nice middle-class neighborhood in West Baltimore. Their street, Druid Hill Avenue was integrated, which means that black and white people lived side by side.

Thurgood's father had a job on the Baltimore & Ohio Railroad, which kept him away from his family for weeks at a time. The money was good, but when William Marshall had a chance to get a job at the local Gibson Island Club, he took it. That club was a highly respected dining club whose members were powerful Washington leaders.

Norma Marshall taught at an all-black Baltimore elementary school. The children at the school were segregated, or separated, which means that only black children went to school there. White children had their own, separate schools. Black children were not allowed, by law, to attend all-white schools. Besides teaching, Norma Marshall was a talented singer and piano player. Sometimes, she performed in local opera and theater productions. Norma was a strong person who did everything for her children. Her strength of character was a strong influence on her youngest son.

Thurgood described himself as "a pretty tough guy," when he was young. When he got in trouble at school, his principal issued him the standard punishment. He put Marshall in a room in the school's basement and made him read the U. S. Constitution. Marshall had to memorize a passage before he could return to class. Marshall was in trouble so often that, by the time he left that school, he had memorized the whole Constitution.

Later in life, Marshall recalled what a puzzling document the Constitution was. Right there in black and white, it was written that everyone had "equal rights." But Marshall knew African-Americans were not treated equally. Nonetheless, those hours of reading the Constitution later helped Marshall make sure that equal justice would someday be the law of the land.

Besides his familiarity with the Constitution, Marshall spent many hours in courtrooms with his father. Though not a formally educated man, William Marshall made it a hobby to follow court cases. Sometimes, he would spend free afternoons in court, with Thurgood by his side. The two would listen to the lawyers present their cases and follow the step-by-step process of a trial. Thurgood later said his father steered him towards a legal career.

Thurgood's parents provided him with a secure upbringing. But they could not protect him from the prejudice that all African-Americans faced in the early 1900s. When Thurgood heard a boy call another boy a "nigger," he ran home and asked his father what it meant. William told him that it was a dirty word, and if anyone ever called him that, "you not only got my permission to fight him—you got my *orders* to fight him."

WRATHFUL MARSHALL

*W*hen Thurgood graduated from high school in 1925, he was determined to continue his education. His older brother was in college, learning to become a doctor. Thurgood's mother hoped her youngest son would become a dentist.

It was not easy for an African-American to get into college in the 1920s. Colleges in the South only allowed white students admission. Most colleges in the North allowed only a few, select black students to attend. Thurgood decided to go to Lincoln University in Pennsylvania, the nation's oldest all-black, all-male college. The college attracted some of the brightest students in the country. Some students came from as far away as Africa and Asia. Thurgood's classmates at Lincoln included Kwame Nkrumah, the future president of Ghana, and Nnamdi Azikiwe, the future president of Nigeria. Another of Marshall's classmates was Cab Calloway, who later became a famous star, singing such popular 1930s songs as "Minnie the Moocher."

In his first year at college, Marshall fell in with the partying crowd. He spent his weekends traveling and playing cards. But he managed to maintain a B average. He read many books by black authors such as W. E. B. Du Bois, Langston Hughes, and Countee Cullen.

While in college, Marshall sometimes went to services at Philadelphia's Cherry Street Memorial Church. When asked about it later, Marshall joked, "We went there because we learned that's where all the cute chicks went." One of the women that went to the church was Vivian Burey, known as "Buster."

Buster was an undergrad student at the University of Pennsylvania. She and Marshall started dating, and were married within a year. They were both 21.

The Marshalls moved into a small apartment and paid their way through college by working part-time jobs. Thurgood was a bellhop and a waiter, and Buster was a secretary. Thurgood was on the debating team and was known as "Wrathful Marshall" because of his impressive skills of argument. By the time he received his B. A. degree, Marshall was convinced that he wanted to become a lawyer.

The Marshalls moved in with Thurgood's parents and started saving money for law school. In 1930, the all-white University of Maryland rejected Marshall's application. Soon, he began his studies at Howard University, a well-regarded college in Washington, D.C. Although the students at the college were mostly African-Americans, the school accepted students of any race.

Marshall put his days of partying behind him. Attending law school was a lifelong dream, so he dug in hard at his studies. Marshall studied so long and so hard that he lost 40 pounds. But at the end of his first year, he was named the top student in his class. This earned him the job as assistant at the Howard Law Library.

At law school, Marshall rubbed shoulders with some of the finest African-American law teachers and students of the day. Many went on to become ground-breaking fighters in the legal battle for African-American equal rights. In a later speech to Howard students, Marshall summed up his no-nonsense attitude about working hard for the cause.

"When you get in a courtroom, you can't just say, 'Please, Mr. Court, have mercy on me because I'm a Negro.' You are in competition with a well-trained white lawyer and you better be at least as good as he is; and if you expect to win, you better be better. If I give you five cases to read overnight, you better read eight. And when I say eight, you read ten. You go that step further and you might make it."

In 1933, Marshall graduated first in his class. Harvard University offered him a scholarship, but he turned it down. He wanted to begin his law practice immediately. Marshall passed his bar exam, the test required by the state to practice law, and opened a law office in Baltimore.

Thurgood Marshall attended Howard University in Washington, D.C.

Chapter 2

Chipping

Away

at the

Wall

"A FREEBIE LAWYER"

*T*he mid-1930s were not a great time for anyone to begin a law practice. The Great Depression was gripping the country. Many people could not even afford meals for their children, let alone lawyers for lawsuits. And it was especially hard for African-American lawyers. When most African-Americans needed a lawyer, they hired white lawyers. After all, the judges, juries, and people they were fighting were usually white. And white juries were already prejudiced against black people. Most African-Americans felt that white lawyers could get more for black people than a black lawyer could. About the only African-Americans who sought out black lawyers were people who were too poor to pay white lawyers.

The first year he was in business, Marshall lost $1,000—a lot of money in 1933. Marshall and his secretary would sit in the office for weeks without a single person coming through the door. Slowly, clients began to appear; people who had been unfairly evicted from their homes; victims of police brutality; and victims of social injustice. Most could not pay, but Marshall turned no one aside. One old woman contacted him because he had earned a reputation as "a freebie lawyer."

Although there was no money involved, Marshall won most of his early cases. Since it was so unusual for an African-American to receive justice in the courts at the time, word of Marshall's skills spread. Before long, his business picked up. Soon, Marshall was representing some large African-American business interests in Baltimore. When Lillie Jackson revived the Baltimore chapter of the National Association for the Advancement of Colored People (NAACP), she asked Marshall to be the lawyer for the organization. The job, like many others, paid nothing, but it was a position of honor for such a young man.

At that time, the NAACP had a reputation for only catering to the needs of wealthier black citizens. Marshall said, "When I was a kid, we said that NAACP stood for National Association for the Advancement of *Certain* People." Marshall meant to change that.

Marshall set out to recruit members for the NAACP. He traveled to neighborhoods, gave speeches, called on business leaders. Soon Marshall was giving hope to people who had lost it long ago.

Marshall organized groups of African-American high school graduates to picket businesses that sold to black people but refused to hire them as workers. When the store owners sued the NAACP, Marshall fought them in court and won.

Thurgood Marshall worked as Chief Counsel for the National Association for the Advancement of Colored People (NAACP).

THE HISTORY OF "SEPARATE BUT EQUAL"

*T*o understand what lawyers such as Thurgood Marshall were up against, it is important to understand the system that they were working within. The U. S. Constitution is the highest law of the land. When it was written in 1789, it included the Bill of Rights, with ten amendments. They guaranteed rights, such as freedom of religion, freedom of the press, and the right to a fair trial.

But when the Constitution was written, it only applied to white men. Women, Native Americans, and African-Americans (who were slaves at the time), had no rights under the Constitution. Some of the men who wrote the Constitution wanted to do away with slavery and include women. But so much time was spent fighting over the issue that there was almost no Constitution. Compromises were made.

The Supreme Court was set up to interpret the Constitution. If a law was made that restricted a right in the Constitution, the Supreme Court could overturn, or do away with it. In 1857, Dred Scott, an African-American slave, asked the Supreme Court to make him a free man. At that time, the Supreme Court said African-Americans did not have the right to freedom because they were property not people. Many people did not agree with that position. Soon after, the United States fought the Civil War in order to, among other things, banish slavery in the United States forever.

In 1857, Dred Scott, an African-American slave, asked the Supreme Court to make him a free man.

African-Americans were made to eat in separate restaurants, use separate public restrooms and sit in separate train station waiting rooms.

The Civil War was a brutal and bloody war, killing hundreds of thousands of people. When it was over, President Abraham Lincoln wanted to change the Constitution to outlaw slavery. Changes to the Constitution are called amendments. It is difficult to change, or amend, the Constitution. But soon the Constitution added the Thirteenth Amendment, ending all slavery, the Fourteenth Amendment, officially making African-Americans citizens of the United States, and the Fifteenth Amendment, allowing African-American men to vote. The last amendment, added in 1870, was supposed to make African Americans legally equal to white people.

Unfortunately, pieces of paper and laws do not change people's attitudes. There was discrimination all over the United States. In the South, especially, African American were not treated equally. They were given separate restaurants, separate public restrooms, and separate waiting rooms in train stations. Soon, signs were placed on everything from drinking fountains to bus seats that said "Colored Only," and "White Only." ("Colored" was a term used to describe African-Americans before the 1960s.)

Thirty years after the slaves were freed, a man named Homer Plessy took a case before the Supreme Court. Plessy was arrested for sitting in a "Whites Only" section of a train. The Supreme Court said that separate was all right, as long as it was equal. In other words, African-Americans could be forced into separate sections of a train as long as those sections were equal to white areas. Thus, "separate- but-equal" became the law of the land. In reality there was separation but there was no equality. Facilities for African-Americans were usually broken, dirty, inferior, or nonexistent.

This "separate but equal" idea was still firmly in place when Thurgood Marshall began the long fight for equality in U. S. courtrooms.

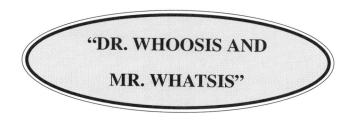

"DR. WHOOSIS AND MR. WHATSIS"

*M*arshall and the NAACP's first order of business together was to organize African-American teachers. They were receiving about half the wages of white teachers. Using the courts and the legal system, Marshall eventually won equal wages for black teachers.

Marshall's next goal was to integrate all-white graduate schools. He started with the University of Maryland, a school that had denied him entrance because of the color of his skin. In several dramatic courtroom battles, Marshall won the right of a black student to attend the University of Maryland law school.

The Maryland Court of Appeals said that the state "must furnish equality of treatment" to black students. This meant that the state had two choices. It could build a school for black students that was equally as good as the white college. Or it could let black students into the University of Maryland. Building a new school would cost too much, so black students were admitted to the all-white college. Marshall was chipping away at the "separate-but-equal" doctrine and this successful court battle was the first step.

Although the taste of victory was sweet, Marshall was still providing his services free of charge. In 1936, one of his former professors at Howard, Charles Houston, asked Marshall if he wanted to become his assistant as first special counsel to the NAACP. The job paid $2,400 a year, a fairly decent sum in the 1930s. Houston said the job was often frustrating, discouraging, and dangerous. Twenty-eight-year-old Marshall jumped at the chance.

For the next several years, Marshall and Houston traveled the South in Marshall's beat-up 1929 Ford, defending the rights of black students and teachers. Since blacks were not allowed in most hotels and restaurants in the South, the two lawyers worked in the car, eating sandwiches and typing legal briefs until the wee hours of the morning.

Little by little, the lawyers chipped away at the wall of segregation. In a Missouri case, the U. S. Supreme Court said that schools must have equal college facilities for African-Americans.

In 1938, Marshall was appointed as head special council for the NAACP. He was 30 years old. He moved to New York City where he took up the job as the country's most important African-American attorney.

Through it all, Marshall retained his down-to-earth style. When he got to the New York offices of the NAACP, he did not like the formal attitude of the people there. Marshall later described it to a *New York Times* reporter: "It was Dr. Whoosis and Mr. Whatsis and all kinds of nonsense like that, bowing and scrapping like an embassy scene. Well, I took a long look and I figured I'd have to bust that stuff up pretty quickly. Believe me, I had them talking first names in nothing time and no more of that formality business."

One of Marshall's first jobs was to oversee the NAACP Legal Defense Fund. The fund was set up to represent African-Americans, at no charge, who had been denied justice because of their race. It was also used to promote educational opportunities for blacks.

MR. CIVIL RIGHTS

*T*he Fifteenth Amendment to the Constitution gave black men the right to vote. (Black and white women were not given the vote until 1920.) Although the Constitution guaranteed African-Americans the right to vote, in the South many laws were enacted to keep blacks from voting. Some states had poll taxes, where a black person had to pay to vote. Many poor people could not afford to pay. Other states had "literacy tests"—long, complicated tests that most people, black or white, could not possibly answer correctly. In Alabama, for instance, black voters were asked to explain "any article of the Constitution to the satisfaction of the voting officials." The few black citizens who could pass the test and pay the tax were then threatened with violence on election day. No more than 3 percent of eligible black people voted in the South in the 1930s.

By 1946, Marshall won several court cases that began to push aside roadblocks to African-American voting rights. That year, he also was awarded the Spingarn Medal, the NAACP's highest award. He was now one of the best-known lawyers in the United States. Soon, the press and the world began to call him "Mr. Civil Rights."

Voting rights aside, many African-Americans still had one of the most basic necessities denied to them—decent housing. In many areas of the United States, no matter how much money a black person had, he or she could not buy a home in a white neighborhood. Again, Marshall fought against discrimination, this time in housing. And again, he won his case before the Supreme Court. In 1948, the Supreme Court outlawed discrimination in housing. Technically, this meant that African-Americans could live in any neighborhood that they wanted.

Of course, these laws were hard to enforce, but this decision meant the law was on the side of equal justice.

Year after year, Marshall whittled away at the "separate-but-equal" doctrine. Each time he proved that facilities for African Americans were not equal, Marshall and the NAACP won another case. But it was tiresome, tedious work, fighting each case on a state-by-state level. And even after courts ordered desegregation, officials found ways of getting around the court orders.

One African-American man, for example, who was studying for a doctorate at the University of Oklahoma, was allowed into the all-white college. But he was forced to listen to lectures outside the open door of the classroom. He had to eat in the cafeteria alone, when no other white students were eating. He also had to sit behind a screen in the library so no white students would see him. This man, George W. McLaurin was a 68-year-old college professor studying for his Ph.D. When Marshall fought this case before the Supreme Court in 1950, he tried to prove that there could not be equality if there was separation. Marshall won, but in a narrow victory that still left the walls of segregation in place.

TEARING DOWN THE WALL IN LITTLE ROCK

*B*y 1952, Thurgood Marshall had been fighting segregation for almost twenty years. Putting in twenty-hour workdays and furiously traveling the country, Marshall only lost three of the twenty-two cases he had argued before the Supreme Court. Still, his fights had not markedly improved the lives of most African-Americans. Still focusing his attention on schools, Marshall knew that there would only be full equality when there was full integration. Black and white students must go to the same schools together.

To prove that there was no equality in African-American schools, Marshall went to Clarendon County, South Carolina. The county's 276 white students had two brick schoolhouses. There was one teacher for every 28 students. The schools offered courses in biology, typing, and bookkeeping. They had flush toilets, cafeterias, and school buses. In contrast, the county's 800 black students had three rickety wooden buildings and one teacher for every 47 children. The schools taught courses in farming and home economics. Students had outdoor toilets and no lunchrooms. Because they had no buses, some students, as young as six years old, were forced to walk five miles to school.

If Marshall won this case, it would prove that unless the schools were fully integrated, there could be no equality. Marshall enlisted the help of Dr. Kenneth B. Clark, a New York City college professor, to help fight his case. Clark, along with his wife, Mamie, used a simple test with dolls to study the effects of segregation on black children.

Clark showed young black children four dolls that were exactly the same, except for color. Two dolls looked like an African-American, the other two looked like white people. When African-American children were asked which dolls were "prettiest" and which dolls were "nicest" most chose the white dolls. When asked which doll looked "bad," most black students chose the African-American doll. About half the children, when asked to pick the doll that looked most like them, picked the white doll.

The results were clear. Separating African-American children gave them a low opinion of themselves. But no one had ever used dolls in a court case before. It was a risky case. Marshall lost in Clarendon County when the county said they would make black schools equal "as soon as possible." On his way out of the courtroom, the county lawyer approached Marshall. He said, "If you ever show up in Clarendon Country again, you're a dead man." Marshall paid him little mind. It was just another one of the dozens of death threats he received every year. Marshall knew the case was heading for the Supreme Court.

On December 9, 1952, the Supreme Court decided to hear the case along with four other school cases the NAACP was fighting—in Delaware, Virginia, the District of Columbia, and Kansas. The cases were lumped together under the title *Brown v. the Board of Education of Topeka*. (The "v." stands for versus, or against.) The trial was long and complicated. Eighty-five sociologists, historians, political scientists, and educators testified. On May 17, 1954, the Supreme Court struck down the separate-but-equal doctrine. Fifty-four years after the court invented the doctrine, the law was declared unconstitutional. All schools in the United States would have to be integrated. Marshall said he was so happy, that he was numb.

Marshall's happiness soon turned to sadness. Shortly after the case, his wife and best friend, Buster, told him she was dying of cancer. Putting aside his law career, Thurgood spent every waking moment at her side until she died in February 1954.

Meanwhile, the victory in the *Brown* decision was the first shot in a major battle. The governor of Virginia stated, "I shall use every legal means at my command to continue segregated schools in Virginia." Soon, the governors of North Carolina and South Carolina joined him. The governor of Georgia said the decision had turned the Constitution into "a mere scrap of paper." The Supreme Court decision in the South was known as "Black Monday."

But when the final decision was handed down on May 31, 1955, the Supreme Court left it up to state courts to integrate the schools. They said this should be done "with all deliberate speed." What this meant is that Marshall and the NAACP would have to go back to each state and fight again for school integration. The state of Georgia said they would fight the case in each of the state's 159 counties. Marshall said that was fine, he'd fight every one of them.

The court's decision was marked with violence in the Deep South. In Mississippi, roving gangs of whites burned down African-American homes and churches. Black leaders who had fought the equality battle were murdered. For the first time, white people who had fought by the side of African-Americans were killed by terrorists. School integration was not going to be easy.

Meanwhile, in late 1955, Marshall began dating the Hawaiian-born Cecilia Suyat, an NAACP secretary. The quiet, even-tempered Sissie was the perfect foil for the dynamic, boisterous Marshall. The couple were married in December. Soon the couple had two sons.

In September 1957, the school integration situation exploded. Nine black students tried to attend school at the all-white Central High School in Little Rock, Arkansas.

In Little Rock, Arkansas, 250 National Guard troops surrounded Central High School. This was to protect the nine African-American students who were finally given the right to attend.

The governor of the state, Orval Fabus, had a different idea. Fabus went on TV the night before school started and announced: "Blood will run in the streets if Negro pupils should attempt to enter Central High School." Fabus said that he would surround the school with National Guardsmen to keep the African-Americans away.

Two-hundred and fifty National Guard troops surrounded Central High the next morning. The students, known as the "Little Rock Nine," planned to go to school together for safety's sake. But one student, 15-year-old Elizabeth Eckford did not have a telephone. She was not told of the plan. When Elizabeth arrived at school alone that morning she was met by armed soldiers and a mob of angry white people. When the mob turned violent, the soldiers did nothing to help her.

Elizabeth fled to a nearby bus stop. The crowd screamed at her and threatened to hang her in a tree. Elizabeth was saved by a white woman who helped her escape. When the other eight black students arrived at the school the National Guard turned them away. President Dwight Eisenhower called Governor Fabus and ordered him to admit the students.

On Monday morning, September 23, the Little Rock Nine finally entered Central High School. A crowd of 1,000 angry white people surrounded the school yelling racist and obscene slogans. Fearing a riot would break out, the students were ordered home. The next morning, Eisenhower ordered 350 federal troops to the school. Each student was assigned a bodyguard. The Little Rock Nine were finally allowed to go to school. Some of the white students accepted the situation rather easily. One of the African-American teenagers, Minniejean Brown, was invited to join the glee club. Some other black students were invited to eat lunch with white students. By the end of the school year, Central High graduated its first African-American student.

Still, racial tensions would not go away. In June, the Little Rock School Board asked for, and received, a two-and-a-half-year delay for integrating the schools. The case eventually ended up before the Supreme Court. The court ordered integration to continue. Fabus refused to give up. He ordered all of the state's racially integrated schools to close. Again, Marshall had to argue the case before the Supreme Court. Finally in 1959, Arkansas' black and white students were allowed to go to school together in peace.

An unidentified boy and woman protest the integration ruling brought down by the Supreme Court. This allowed African-Americans to attend the same schools as whites.

Chapter 3

The President's Call

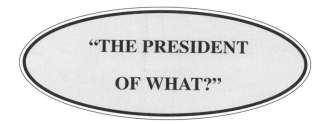

"THE PRESIDENT

OF WHAT?"

*F*or the next several years, Marshall fought for school integration in Louisiana, Alabama, Virginia, South Carolina, and Texas. Marshall also argued cases to integrate public beaches, public housing, buses and trains, and sports arenas. In several of these cases, Marshall worked with civil rights leader Dr. Martin Luther King, Jr.

In November 1960, John F. Kennedy was elected the thirty-fifth president of the United States. In September 1961, he nominated Thurgood Marshall for a judgeship on the Court of Appeals for the Second Circuit.

The federal judicial system is made up of three levels. The lowest level is the district court. If someone loses a case in a district court, he or she may appeal the decision to a Court of Appeals. There are eleven Appeals Courts, each for a different region of the country.

The Second Circuit Court, to which Marshall was nominated, covered the states of Vermont, New York, and Connecticut. If someone loses a case in a Court of Appeals, he or she may ask that the decision be overturned by the highest court, the Supreme Court. This is very rare. Because of the huge number of cases before the Supreme Court, it only agrees to hear a small percentage of cases. Usually the decision of the Court of Appeals is final. When Marshall was confirmed to sit on the Court of Appeals, he was on one of the second highest courts in the land.

As a federal judge, Marshall ruled on a wide variety of cases. In four years, the Supreme Court did not overrule one of the 98 cases he decided. Now, Marshall no longer had to fight noisy court battles for the smallest elements of justice. As a federal judge, his word became the law.

One day in June 1965, Marshall was having lunch with a friend. An aide arrived with a message: "The president is on the phone."

"The president of what?" Marshall asked.

"Of the United States, sir," the aide answered.

Marshall picked up the phone and spoke to President Lyndon Johnson. Johnson wanted Marshall to become the solicitor general of the United States. This was the third highest legal position, after attorney general and assistant attorney general. Johnson told Marshall: "I want people to walk down the hall at the Justice Department and see a black man sitting there." Soon, Marshall went to Washington, D.C., to begin his new job.

As solicitor general, Marshall would argue the nation's top cases before the Supreme Court. This official directs all cases in which the United States has an interest. The solicitor general also decides which of the hundreds of cases the Justice Department will ask the Supreme Court to hear. Marshall was the first African-American to hold this post.

But taking the position meant a cut in pay for Marshall. It also meant giving up a lifetime appointment as a federal judge. Marshall could only hold the solicitor general's post as long as Johnson was president. But Marshall took the job. When asked by reporters why he had made this "sacrifice," Marshall answered, "because the president asked me to." Then he added, "I believe that in this time, especially, we do what our government requests of us. Negroes have made great advances in government and I think it's time they started making some sacrifices."

Between 1965 and 1967, Marshall won 14 out of the 19 cases he argued before the Supreme Court. Most of them dealt with civil rights and privacy issues. As Marshall approached his sixtieth birthday, the country had changed remarkably. Integration and equality were encoded in law. Racial discrimination was illegal. Voting rights were guaranteed. These new laws and court decisions would take years to actually change people's attitudes. But for those changing times, the hand of Thurgood Marshall was on the rudder of the ship steering the country towards equality.

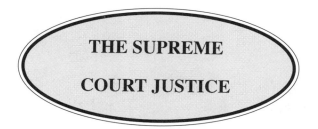

THE SUPREME

COURT JUSTICE

*O*n June 13, 1967, Thurgood Marshall and Lyndon Johnson faced down a battery of TV cameras that were waiting in the White House Rose Garden. Johnson had just asked Marshall to serve on the Supreme Court. The president told the nation: "I believe it is the right thing to do, the right time to do it, the right man and the right place. I believe that he [Marshall] has already earned his place in history, but I think it will be greatly enhanced by his service on the Court."

Thurgood Marshall takes his place in history on the Supreme Court.

The reaction in the African-American community to Marshall's appointment was one of joy. After almost 200 years, a black man, a grandson of a slave, would serve on the country's highest court. And Marshall's appointment contained another bittersweet twist of history. The last Maryland-born justice on the Supreme Court was Roger Taney, chief justice from 1836 to 1864. Taney was the justice who had ruled on the famous Dred Scott case in 1857. In that decision, Taney had said that African-Americans were "property not people" and had no rights under the Constitution. Now, more than a century after that fateful decision, Thurgood Marshall was taking his place in history on the Supreme Court.

In a later interview, Johnson said he nominated Marshall for the sake of black children. "All over America that day," Johnson recalled, "Negro parents looked at their children a little differently, thousands of mothers looked across the breakfast table and said, 'Now, maybe this will happen to my child someday.'"

On October 2, 1967, Thurgood Marshall took the oath of office.

Marshall continued his long battle against school segregation from the nation's highest court. In 1971, the court ruled that schools could use buses to end segregation. If necessary, school boards could bus black children to white schools and white children to black schools. This stirred quite a controversy. White parents did not want their children to go to schools across town. Many parents pulled their children from public schools.

In 1972 President Richard Nixon spoke out against busing. Nixon backed up his words when he appointed two conservative justices to the Supreme Court, William Rehnquist and Lewis Powell. These justices moved the court to a more conservative direction, causing some setbacks for African-American issues. Suddenly, Marshall found himself on the losing end of many court decisions.

Since Supreme Court justices are appointed for life, there was constant discussion of Marshall's age and how much longer he would be able to serve. One time when Marshall was sick and in the hospital, a doctor told him that President Nixon wanted to see his medical reports. The doctor said that Nixon wanted to see how close to death Marshall was, so he could start the process of naming a more conservative judge. Marshall took the folder of medical records from the doctor and scrawled two words across it in large black script — "**NOT YET!**"

When Ronald Reagan was elected president in 1980, he vowed to make the Supreme Court even more conservative. And, as promised, Reagan's new court appointees swung the court further away from the issues that Marshall cherished the most. But when asked whether he was discouraged by the court's conservative tilt, Marshall said he was not. He said he had seen a lot worse than could be imagined nowadays. Marshall said that the changes wrought by the civil rights movement would prove more lasting than the reactions against them. He added that "hand wringing is a futile response to challenge."

By the mid-1980s, Marshall suffered many of the effects of old age. Over the years he had heart attacks, bronchitis, blood clots, hearing loss, and glaucoma. Still he refused to retire. One time he told a clerk, "If I die, prop me up and keep on voting."

*Thurgood Marshall dedicated fifty years of
his life to the betterment of all humanity.*

"I'M FALLING APART!"

*O*n June 27, 1991, Marshall finally announced his retirement. When ask why, by reporters, he crowed, "I'm old! I'm falling apart!" After dedicating fifty years of his life to public service, Thurgood Marshall stepped down from the Supreme Court. Four days later, President George Bush nominated conservative federal Appeals Court justice Clarence Thomas to replace Marshall.

On January 24, 1993, Thurgood Marshall died. He was 84 years old. Some of the most famous people in the world attended his funeral. They all came to pay tribute to this great man of word and deed.

Marshall's body lay in state in the Great Hall of the Supreme Court—the same place Abraham Lincoln's casket had rested. From 10 in the morning until 10 in the evening a steady flow of people filed past the casket. Over 20,000 mourners came to pay their last respects to Marshall.

There are many great women and men who have fought the battle for African-American rights. Some have fought at state capitals holding picket signs. Some have fought on street corners holding Bibles. But Thurgood Marshall took the battle from the streets to the courtroom, holding the words of the Constitution close to his heart. And he gave new meaning and life to those words. In court case after court case, Marshall coaxed an entire nation to come to grips with the wrongs in its past.

When the Constitution was written, women, Native Americans, and African-Americans were not part of its first three words. Thanks to Thurgood Marshall, today everyone in the United States may be counted as "We the people."

GLOSSARY

Amendment - a change or addition.

Conservative - a person who is opposed to certain changes in a political system.

Desegregation - ending or stopping a law or practice that separates and isolates people because of their race.

Discrimination - denying people housing, jobs, or equal rights because of their race, sex, religion, or skin color.

Integrate - to make occupancy of a place open to all races.

Ku Klux Klan (KKK) - a secret organization that uses violence and terror against black people and other minorities. Members of the Ku Klux Klan were white pointy hoods over their heads and burn crosses at their meetings.

Prejudice - dislike or hatred of people because of their race, sex, religion, or skin color; an unfavorable opinion formed about a person or situation without complete knowledge of the facts.

Racism - the dislike or hatred of people because of their race or ethnic background.

Segregate - to separate. In the South, laws kept black people segregated from white people.

Unconstitutional - not agreeable to the Constitution of the United States.

INDEX

jB
MARSHALL

Kallen, Stuart

Thurgood Marshall

480713

DISCARD

$14.96

DATE			